Journeys

Journeys

Steve Gannaway

Illustrated by Deborah Thompson

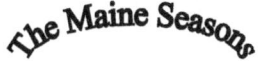

Copyright © 2010 Steven K. Gannaway
All Rights Reserved

All rights reserved. No part of this book may be used or reproduced in any manner whatsoever without written permission except in the case of brief quotations embedded in critical articles or book reviews.

ISBN: 978-0-9830047-0-7

The author may be contacted at
maine.seasons@hotmail.com

The Maine Seasons
12 Lucerne St.
Springvale, ME 04083

Cover photo by Mary Gillings Gannaway,

"The Innkeeper," "The Shepherds," and "The Shepherd Boy," in earlier forms, were used in Gannaway family Christmas cards (1989, 2005, 2008, respectively).
"Journey to the Valley of Elah" and "Journey to the Source of Mercy" have been previously published, in earlier forms, at FanStory.com.

Dedicated to
Mary, Rick and Sorieya.

Thank you for your love and support.
S. G.

Contents

Preface   ix

Old Testament: Journeys of Obedience and Trust
Journey to Mount Ararat (Noah)   3
Journey to Mount Moriah (Abraham)   9
Journey to Nineveh (Jonah)   15
Journey down Mount Sinai (Moses)   21
Journey to the Temple of Dagon (Samson)   23
Journey to the Valley of Elah (David)   29

The Birth of the Christ: Journeys to Bethlehem
Mary   39
The Innkeeper   47
The Shepherds   51
The Shepherd Boy   55
The Magi   (Told by Balthazar)   59

New Testament: Model of a Disciple's Journey
Journey to the Font of Mercy
        (The Woman Caught in Adultery)   69
Journey to Conversion (Saul)   73
Journey to Integrity (Zacchaeus)   79

Journey to Church
    (The Elamite Tells his Story)   87
Journey to the Lord's Table
    (Told by John the Apostle)   91
Journey through Death to New Life,
    (Lazarus, Told by Martha and Mary)   95

Your Journey   103
Landmark One: Mount Ararat (sample)   107

Preface

The poems in *Journeys* do not represent a new translation or version of the Bible. Think of me as a storyteller rather than a linguist or theologian. Good stories abound in the Bible. In *Journeys*, I have the pleasure of telling you seventeen of them.

As I tell the stories, I make every effort to remain true to their essence. However, it is a storyteller's prerogative to fill in details where the Bible leaves them open. Here are two examples.

The first comes from the life and death of Samson (page 23). When captured, he is blinded by the blades of Philistine knives. In his dying act, Samson wipes out the leaders of this enemy of Israel. It would be a nice touch if a surprising and generous God restored Samson's sight prior to his death. The Bible does not tell us this, but a storyteller may.

The second example comes from Luke's Gospel in a backdoor sort of way. It is Luke we must thank for most of our knowledge of Jesus' birth. He writes that Mary's first-born Son was wrapped in swaddling clothes and placed in the manger because there had been no room at the inn (Luke 2:7). The innkeeper does not even rate a mention. There must have been one; it is something no self-respecting inn would go without.

To a teller of tales, this lack of information is a blank check. What sort of man was the innkeeper, and how did he experience the nativity? Or, was the innkeeper a woman? Starting on page 47, I will tell you.

If my retelling of a story contains details you do not remember, do not panic. By all means, though, pick up your Bible and check. The Bible is the inspired Word of God, read it frequently.

I am grateful to Deborah Thompson whose illustrations enrich this book. Take time to look deeply into them. Like icons of the Eastern Church, they draw you into the story, into the encounter with God.

It is impossible to thank by name all who read and critiqued parts of this manuscript at various points.

Their number is too great. However, like an Academy Award recipient, I have my list and I will thank as many as I can before they yank me from the stage.

Martha Mountford was encouraging and very helpful in the book's infancy. The regulars at the Sanford Writers Group were unfailingly supportive and encouraging: Bill, Bob, Gladys and Hazel. Thanks to my siblings and their spouses who were not only supportive, but on short notice, with an imminent deadline, undertook the job of proofreading the text: Tony, Susie, Scott, Jill, Chris, Connie, Rich and especially Lynn and my mother-in-law, Madeleine, who read drafts of this book with a wonderfully critical eye. My son, Rick, was my technical support department. My daughter, Sorieya, encouraged me in my writing by sharing hers with me. Both have immeasurably enriched my life and given me a reason to write.

Finally, and most important, I thank God for taking the improbable and making it reality. In 1984, I was a teacher from North Dakota, in my last summer at Providence College, finishing a Masters Degree. That same summer, He brought Mary Gillings from Maine to Providence for a course on the New Testament. It took just one day of conversation at Old Sturbridge Village to plant love's seed. For twenty-five years, she has been my most ardent supporter, a reliably honest critic, the love of my life, and my wife. Thank you.

Old Testament:

Journeys of Obedience and Trust

Journey to Mount Ararat (Noah)

It had begun so long before,
That Noah scarce could count the years.
At journey's end, on land once more,
His memories brought grateful tears.

The depth of evil on the earth
Led God to shape a drastic plan
To cleanse and grant the world rebirth,
Preserving Noah and his clan.

Above floodwaters, they would float,
So, with his sons, who numbered three,
The man began to build a boat,
Far off from river, lake and sea.

Not they alone would dodge this woe,
But, as the ark grew broad and high,
They searched the trees, they searched below,
For animals from land and sky.

Inhabitants of nearby towns
Engaged in laughing mockery,
Describing Noah's sons as clowns,
Deriding their menagerie.

But they, in terror, filled the plain
As heaven's face grew dark.
Then came the rain, torrential rain;
The old man watched God seal the ark.

The holds were full, no space remained
For them or for the sins they bore.
Old Noah, standing, wan and pained,
Watched cleansing tears from heaven pour.

The ark first shifted in its cradle,
And started rising on day four.
Great waves then freed the floating stable,
While rain continued all the more.

They fed their guests within the ark,
Avoiding beaks and teeth and claws.
With torches twinkling in the dark,
The small band's toils knew no pause.

The skies stormed forty days, then ceased.
No more rain drummed decks with sound;
No more wind howled west to east;
No more waves leapt all around.

There was much sighing in relief
Within the cloistered little band.
They trusted Noah's firm belief
In God who would restore the land.

Through endless days, they gently swayed,
Before a first small shudder came.
Then Noah bent his knees and prayed,
Grateful words that blessed God's name.

The days were marked by frequent bumps
Until the ark was lodged in place.
In time, they saw the first tree stumps,
Tops swept away without a trace.

Prodigious was their joy when they
At last, beheld the naked ground
On which the ark had come to stay,
By size and weight securely bound.

They looked out, restless, for a sign
That they might leave and celebrate.
An itch to move ran up each spine,
But Noah said that they must wait.

Their guests displayed a restlessness
That matched their own at this delay.
All watched with hope the dove's egress
When Noah sent her on her way.

Hours later, when the dove returned,
She held the sign for which they yearned.

Their eyes dipped low when she returned;
She had found no nesting place.
But to his sons, old Noah turned,
"Trust God. We rest in His embrace."

So, Noah waited six days still,
Then he again the dove released.
When she returned, all felt a chill,
She held a branch brought from the East.

The sons were anxious six days more,
But Noah waited patiently.
The seventh day, as twice before
Their father set the small dove free.

In vain, they waited through the night
To hear their scout call in the dark,
But having found a nesting site,
Her future lay beyond the ark.

Then Noah said the time had come
To offer God their thanks and praise,
Who had not let the clan succumb
To raging waters through those days.

The ark's door fueled long arcs of fire
As Noah offered sacrifice.
When flames went down, he left the pyre,
And beheld a paradise.

With joy, the sons heard Noah's words:
"From pens and cages on the ark,
Largest mammals to smallest birds,
Must be released and disembark."

God gave a blessing and command
To those preserved while heaven stormed
"Go! Multiply. Subdue the land.
For in God's image you were formed."

No more, vowed God, would He destroy,
By such a flood, the earth below—
A pledge renewed, to Noah's joy,
In rainbows that the rains bestow.

Read it in the Bible: Genesis 6:11 — 8:22

Journey to Mount Moriah (Abraham)

Long ago, a man named Abram
Heard the voice of God Most High,
"Leave your people for the land
I will set before your eye."

A promise with this call was paired,
"If you believe and trust in me,
You, though childless and white-haired,
Will have a great posterity."

Though Sarai, Abram's wife, was old,
Devoid of hope to end her shame,
Still, Abram did as he was told;
Abraham and Sarah they became.

She was childless, but he believed;
Two dozen times the sheep were shorn,
Then faith's fulfillment he received,
When his and Sarah's son was born.

Through all the years, they still believed,
Then faith's fulfillment they received.

Years later, in the depth of night,
The voice returned from long before.
The voice of God, Lord of Might,
This time a painful mandate bore.

"Go, offer on Moriah's slope,
Upon an altar built with stone,
The son I gave you, bound with rope;
Thus will your love for God be shown."

As directed, Abraham
Rose up before the night was done,
Woke Isaac gently as a lamb,
This gift of God, his only son.

The servants wakened in the night,
Abraham, with signs, directed
To gather kindling and tie tight
On an ass what they collected.

Leaving Sarah, whose heart would have burst,
They journeyed three days in the heat.
Isaac saw the mountain first,
Leaping up with youthful feet.

As dawn first brushed the sky with light,
The man took from the donkey's back
The load his servants had bound tight,
And had his son take up the pack.

With the servants charged to stay
Where the mountain stood in view,
He and Isaac turned away—
They continued, just the two.

As they walked the winding track,
To his father, Isaac turned,
"You tied the branches to my back,
But, in the flames, what will be burned?"

"God is good and will provide,"
Said the father to his son,
As they reached the mountainside,
Glowing under midday sun.

They climbed up to the rocky site,
Where Abraham then toiled alone.
He, while mourning his son's plight,
Built the altar stone by stone.

He heaped the branches on the altar,
With tears secured the boy on top,
Grabbed his dagger and did not falter.
He raised it, ready, slashed down, "Stop!"

He did not hear the heavens speak,
But, even as toothed lightening sprayed,
Angelic hosts besieged the peak
And gripped the hand that gripped the blade.

"Abraham," the voice went on.
"Lord, my God, I serve you here."
"Do not lay your hand upon
Your young son or cause him fear.

"It is clear you love the Lord.
Since you heeded this command,
You will have the blessing stored:
Offspring countless as the sand."

Abraham, slashing with his knife,
Freed Isaac from the knotted cord.
He wished, in thanks for his son's life,
To make an offering to the Lord.

He saw in a nearby thicket,
A ram that by its horns was caught.
Abraham seized hold, then killed it,
And sacrificed what God had brought.

They spoke together as fire burned,
Smoke mingling with the prayers they cried.
"Long ago, my son, I learned
That, in our need, God will provide."

Read it in the Bible: Genesis 12:1-9; 21:1-7; 22:1-18

The fish that caught him in the sea,
Now set the chastened prophet free.

Journey to Nineveh (Jonah)

The Word of God had come to Jonah,
A prophet in God's name.
It sent the man to Nineveh
To herald heavenly flame.

To cross that city took three days
And Jonah's fear was great.
So, boarding ship to flee God's gaze,
He hid down with the freight.

Evading swords the sky slashed down,
The vessel ducked and leapt,
While, heedless that they all might drown,
The fleeing prophet slept.

The crew tossed cargo overboard,
Then woke him from his sleep
"Pray! Call upon your God, the Lord,
To save us from the deep."

"On whose account are we to die?"
The sailors asked each other.
"Which god are we to pacify?
Let the lots uncover."

When, to Jonah, fell the lot,
He said, "I flee the Lord;
You must preserve yourselves and ought
To throw me overboard."

Exhausting other options first,
They turned reluctantly,
And seized the prophet, then, headfirst,
Consigned him to the sea.

Seaward, the flailing prophet spun.
The crew cried to the Lord,
"Forgive, forgive what we have done.
Show mercy," they implored.

As waves grabbed Jonah hungrily,
He madly gasped for air,
Convinced each time his head poked free,
That Death would find him there.

The Lord, though, sent a giant fish
As waves reduced their roll.
The prophet seemed a dainty dish—
It swallowed Jonah whole.

To his surprise, the prophet found
He lived; he was not dead.
He filled the dark with joyful sound
To God Whom he had fled.

"I sought the Lord in my distress—
He came and answered me.
I offer prayers in gratefulness;
The saving God is He."

Through three long nights and three dark days,
He prayed to God, his Lord,
Until, beneath the sun's bright rays,
The fish spat out its hoard.

God spoke within the midday blaze,
"To the city, go and say,
'God's anger will, in forty days,
Burn Nineveh away.'"

Jonah left without delay
For the massive city,
Where God's warning he conveyed
Concerning coming calamity.

With open ears, citizens heard
The message Jonah brought.
The king as well received this word
And mercy he, too, sought.

To all the places where he reigned
He had his heralds proclaim,
"All evil here must be constrained;
May God save us from our shame."

Upon seeing their reaction,
God turned his wrath aside,
But the Lord's compassion
Offended Jonah's pride.

His prophecy a failure,
For that was Jonah's thought,
He became a doleful figure.
Depressed, he cared for naught.

God caused a plant to quickly grow,
To ward off sun and heat;
From Jonah's place, reclined below,
He felt despair retreat.

But worms devoured its insides through
Before the next day's dawn.
It crumpled when the east wind blew;
His shelter now was gone.

The prophet gave an anguished cry
For the plant now at his feet.
"Take my life. Just let me die,"
Moaned Jonah in defeat.

Gently God spoke to the man,
"You mourn a plant you did not sow,
For which you did not till the land,
And did not cause to grow.

"Should I not compassion show
To thousands in this city?
They, as well, must come to know
The measure of my mercy."

He praised the gracious God of all,
As humbly, he agreed.
When next he heard the Lord's voice call,
Jonah was quick to heed.

Read it in the Bible: The Book of Jonah

Moses felt his rage ignite;
He flung the tablets left and right.

Journey down Mount Sinai (Moses)

"Enough!" He cried upon the sight
Of sacrificial flames alight,
A calf that glistened goldenly,
The people dancing rowdily;
And Moses felt his rage ignite.

He flung the tablets left and right.
He smashed the calf, with all his might.
To Aaron, blaming franticly,
"Enough!" He cried.

He tried to set the camp aright,
Then climbed again up Sinai's height,
For plague had struck camp suddenly;
He sought God's mercy ardently.
God mourned His people struck by blight,
"Enough!" He cried.

Read it in the Bible: Exodus 32

When he was peacefully asleep,
Delilah sheared him like a sheep.

Journey to the House of Dagon (Samson)

I.   Prologue
When gathered tribes of Israel
Within the Promised Land,
Felt threats from neighbor nations swell
Beyond what they could stand,

The Lord would search within the clan
For one the tribe could know
As judge and hero for a span,
To fight against their foe.

The birth of Samson was foretold:
An angel sent from God
Brought to a woman thought too old
A pledge that left her awed.

For she had never had a child
And thought she never would;
But now on her the Lord had smiled
And promised motherhood.

II. Samson the Judge
At birth, she gave her son to God,
A thorny, fragrant rose.
Throughout the lands of Dan he trod,
With Philistines as foes.

He was a Nazirite for life,
And thus his locks of hair,
That never knew the blade of knife,
Gave Samson strength most rare.

This gift of might made him the bane
Of Philistines he fought—
He gladly left the men in pain,
Their women he then sought.

But mighty Samson finally fell
For eyes like ebony pools,
Through which Delilah cast her spell
On men and other fools.

"Such might," she said, "I have not seen.
From where does it arise?"
Not trusting her, a Philistine,
Three times he gave her lies.

"With seven bowstrings one might bind
My strength and hold me tight,"
But they were beaten and maligned
Who tried it late that night.

He said he could be held by ropes,
Each new and never used,
Then tore those cords that bore their hopes,
Less angry than amused.

So she, the third time, sought his doom,
By weaving Samson's hair
Into the webbing of a loom,
To trap him in her lair.

But Samson woke and freed his head,
Then rose to fight her men.
They quickly fled the tent instead,
Although they numbered ten.

When tears had pried his secret free,
Delilah had him shorn.
His hair and strength thus came to be
As when he first was born.

Now Samson fought his foes in vain;
With knives, they took his sight.
They made him labor grinding grain
Throughout each day and night.

III.   To the Temple of Dagon
Since Dagon of the Philistines,
Their god, had brought success,
The nation's leaders planned by means
Of sacrifice to stress

And praise Great Dagon's mighty ways.
For Samson now was weak,
And clan chiefs traveled days to gaze
On Terror rendered Meek.

To Dagon's temple he was led,
As crowds began to swell.
Derision poured on Samson's head,
Like rain on Noah fell.

Blind Samson turned and asked the boy,
Not letting his hand go,
"Please lead me, son, as one last joy,
Before the portico."

The boy led Samson up between
The pillars made of wood,
Supporting roof and mezzanine,
On which three thousand stood.

The Hebrew whispered like a dove
As he released the lad,
"Find shelter from the roof above,
If any may be had."

IV.   Vengeance
Head bowed, he stood within their sight,
Taunts flying from his foes.
But, placing hands to left, to right,
God's thorny, fragrant rose

Called out, "O God, return my might.
Lord, listen to my plea.
Permit me vengeance for the sight,
They took away from me."

He raised blind eyes as strength returned
And like a lion roared.
The Philistines, though not concerned,
Still watched with one accord.

Perceiving Samson's clear intent,
His persecutors jeered.
But, seeing rage so fiercely spent,
Their joy soon disappeared.

His arms became as iron beams,
His sinews, steel cables
That tore at tortured temple seams,
And toppled gilded gables.

The Philistine rejoicing ceased
When Dagon's statue creaked.
As pillars toppled west and east,
All but the bravest shrieked.

The roof of stone and wood caved in,
With those who had stood there
Now calling out, a growing din,
To Dagon in despair.

The boy, where he could safely see,
Watched Dagon's statue fall
And shatter on the shrine's debris,
But Samson still stood tall.

V.   Peace at Last
The Hebrew smiled, for he could see;
God gave him back his sight,
Then he collapsed in the debris,
His foes on left and right.

Read it in the Bible: Judges 13 – 16

Journey to the Valley of Elah (David)

It was an age of clashing arms,
With Israel at war.
The king conscripted men from farms
Then canvassed towns for more.

The oldest three of Jesse's boys
Joined the army of Saul.
His sons were Jesse's greatest joys;
He feared that they would fall.

Five other sons made Jesse glad,
David the youngest one.
He lacked the brawn his brothers had,
But was the boldest son.

His father's sheep placed in his trust,
Young David watched with care,
Protecting them, as shepherds must,
From threats that might be there.

When Jesse called him from the hill,
The chore was no surprise;
His brothers' needs he must fulfill,
By bringing them supplies.

While loaded down with grain and cheese,
He sought his brothers out,
That Jesse's worry he might ease
And pacify his doubt.

When David reached the Valley Elah,
Both armies were in sight;
Saul's soldiers raised the cheer, "Hurrah!"
In ranks, prepared to fight.

A hush. All watched a Philistine
Stride forward from the rear.
A mountainous man like none had seen;
He held a treelike spear.

More daunting still, his leather belt
With giant, bloodstained blade.
Saul's troops could feel their courage melt,
Their boldness quickly fade.

"Your soldiers are not men, but crawl
Like slugs away from me,"
Goliath taunted, standing tall,
As Israel turned to flee.

David was staggered at the sight
And, to his brothers' dismay,
He asked aloud, "Will no one fight?"
They said. "Watch what you say."

To his brothers, he did not yield,
Instead, the youth insisted,
"It shames our God to flee the field!"
The three, though, still resisted,

"You saw Goliath, tall and broad,
What man can stand against?"
"The giant defies the Living God,"
The youth replied, incensed.

"I will, with God's help, end this shame,"
His eyes intense and black.
"You must go home; this is no game,"
The brothers bellowed back,

But, David's words were brought to Saul,
Who called him to his tent.
The youth displayed no fear at all,
Nor strayed from his intent.

Young David, measured by Saul's eyes
Was lithe and wiry strong,
But faced with so much greater size,
He would not last for long.

"Boy," said Saul, "it is quite plain,
You are too young to fight.
Though you are brave, it is not sane
To face that giant's might."

Said David, "While watching sheep by night,
Bear and lion I have slain.
Now, with God's right hand, I will smite
Goliath on the plain."

Relenting, Saul gave his command,
"My armor you shall wear."
Said David, "No. I scarce could stand.
To God I trust my care."

He left the armor and the sword,
Snatched up his shepherd's staff,
And headed toward the Philistine horde
To still the giant's laugh.

He stopped and reached into a brook
To choose a small, smooth stone
Four more stones the young man took,
Then stood and walked alone.

Of God's help, he was certain
His eyes were free of fear.
Goliath's face began to darken;
His lips curled in a sneer.

"Is this the best that Saul could do?
A child armed with a stick?
Boy, though I feed the birds with you,
Fear not, I will be quick."

The youth called back, "You scoff at me;
By sword and spear you stand.
But God, whose might you soon will see,
Has placed you in my hand."

The armies stood expectantly,
The challenge now complete.
Goliath trotted eagerly
On thunderous giant feet.

The pouch of stones at David's waist
Swung gently with his stride.
He plucked one stone and without haste
He tossed his staff aside.

To his belt again he dipped,
Retrieved his leather sling,
And in its pocket deftly slipped
The stone he planned to fling.

He whipped his sling, the stone let fly;
He saw his aim was true.
It struck the giant like an eye
Between the other two.

Though David's stone was small in size,
It struck between the giant's eyes.

Goliath managed one more stride,
Though reeling from the stone,
Then, like a living landslide,
He tumbled, rolled, lay prone.

Saul's troops, their courage now restored,
Awaited word to go;
David seized Goliath's sword,
And gave it with one blow.

Saul's men through Elah's valley spread,
And Philistines, put to rout,
Left goods and bodies as they fled,
And sought an exit route.

David fought no more that day
But waited for his brothers;
At last, he saw them far away
With spoils like all the others.

Success caused anger to abate
As he embraced each brother,
And, leaving them to celebrate,
Returned to father and mother.

Read it in the Bible: 1 Samuel 17

The Birth of the Christ:

Journeys to Bethlehem

Mary

Just fourteen was Mary then,
Pledged to Joseph, a carpenter;
Quietly she was sewing when
Something wondrous happened to her.

As Mary worked, she could not know,
An angel was to visit,
But breeze outside began to blow,
Becoming something exquisite.

She was startled by a visitor,
Gabriel, glowing like the sun.
He said that God had favored her
And chosen her to bear His Son.

She asked how such a thing could be
And he explained, God's Spirit could
Pass over her as soundlessly
As shadows of her mother would.

"The Child that would be born to you
Would be holy, God's own Son."
She said, "I am God's servant true,
So, as you say, let it be done."

Gabriel said one thing more,
That, barren and advanced in years,
Her cousin conceived six months before;
Her eyes filled up with happy tears.

It was suggested that she stay
Mary was patiently insistent.
She was needed without delay,
Though her cousin's home was distant.

Elizabeth cried out with joy
When Mary came into her view;
Her soon-to-be-born little boy
Leapt in joyful greeting, too.

Three months, she helped Elizabeth
Until after John was born.
Mary then returned to Nazareth,
Arriving weary and foot-worn.

Her pregnancy was clear to see
And hurtful stories started spreading.
Joseph, gently and quietly,
Made plans to cancel the wedding.

But Gabriel came to him by night
And spoke within a dream,
"You worry over Mary's plight,
But God is acting to redeem."

The angel went on, "Mary bears
The Son of God inside her womb,
You may marry her without these cares.
Open heart and home to make her room.

Then, from Caesar came a decree
Through all lands that there be a count
Of people in each clan, each family,
And determine their tax amount.

Since Joseph was of David's line,
To Bethlehem they had to go,
But paths at times were serpentine,
And hilly roads made travel slow.

Joseph walked the donkey Mary rode,
Nazareth, Samaria, and on,
Mary shared his pain as Joseph strode
From dawn until sun's light was gone.

Her Child had grown week by week;
Now, day by day, discomfort grew,
But no complaint did Mary speak,
Though Joseph watched her face and knew.

Mary shared his pain as Joseph strode
And led the donkey which she rode.

Through Bethany and five miles more,
At last the town of Bethlehem.
It was day's end and she was sore,
So, Joseph sought a place for them.

He checked each inn they passed in town.
Said many keepers of an inn,
"I really hate to turn you down,
But I have no room within."

One man added, "I am afraid,
There is no space on bed or floor—
Like sheathes they are arrayed,
Tightly packed, no room for more."

An innkeeper at last they found
Who, though he had for them no space,
Added as they turned around,
"Behind the inn, a sheltered place,

A stable, if you wish to check…"
"We, thank you, sir," said Joseph sighing.
Her arms around the donkey's neck,
Mary waited, softly crying.

Behind the inn they sought the stable
And found a cave dug in the hill,
A hay-filled manger, small wood table,
And donkeys, quiet and still.

Beyond the reach of bright star light,
Joseph made a bed of hay.
Uncomfortably, deep in the night,
Awake and praying, Mary lay.

He gently wiped her face to soothe her,
Then Joseph sat nearby to wait;
He soon fell deeply into slumber;
His exhaustion was so great.

The time arrived, but brought no fear,
As Mary did what must be done.
She did not see the angels near,
Until with joy she held her son.

A little later from outside,
She heard the rustling sound of feet;
She stood, with Joseph at her side,
And greeted shepherds with their sheep.

Nervous, respectful and eager,
And not knowing what to say,
The shepherds slowly approached her
And saw the manger where He lay.

When they found they were not spurned
The shepherds gladly told their tale:
From glorious angels they had learned
That God had reached out through the veil.

These men, like all in Israel,
Awaited God's Anointed One;
Now, joy like rain from heaven fell,
For they had found Him in her Son.

Surprises came from every side,
The shepherds' tale was but the start,
And Mary kept these things inside
To ponder often in her heart.

Read it in the Bible: Luke 1:5 — 2:20

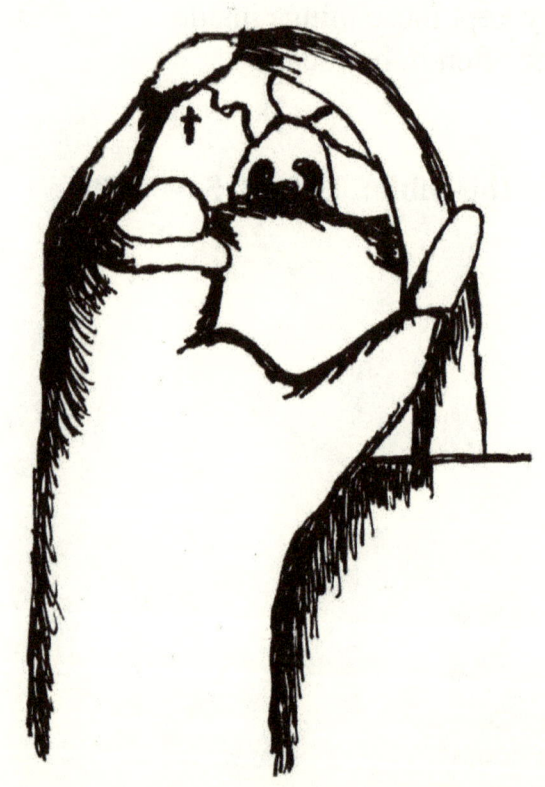

The keeper stretched his arms apart,
And felt joy welling in his heart.

The Innkeeper

The man wore whiskers long and white,
With curls on curls, like fleece of sheep.
His bright eyes glimmered like star light
With joy that never seemed to sleep.

His voice resounded as if drawn
From some deep cistern housed within;
And like matching skies, dusk and dawn,
His laughter was its twin.

In stature, very short and stout
Was this man who kept the inn,
Who first reacted with a shout,
Then gentler, answered once again.

"Neither bed, nor space on the floor
Have I available for you.
I have no room for any more,
I fear, not even for just two."

The keeper eyed the man who stood,
Leaning wearily at his door.
The innkeeper sighed and wished he could
Just clear a little bit of floor.

Behind the man, inside the gate,
A dusty, sweat-streaked donkey bore
A pregnant girl whose Child could wait,
He was sure, not many hours more.

"Please, can you find for her a bed?
Perhaps, a little bit of floor?"
With weary gestures still he pled,
As he had done at inns before.

The innkeeper, unthinking, tugged his beard,
But his fingers caught in the curls,
In his mind, images appeared
And thoughts of his two little girls.

"While it is neither clean nor new,
There is a stable in the back.
Though not much, it will shelter you.
It is not far, along the track."

"It was the best that I could do,"
He muttered softly to the night,
And thoughtfully he watched the two,
Until the path took them from sight.

Three men already claimed his bed,
So, in a small back upper room,
The keeper joined eight men instead,
Squeezed in as if they shared one womb.

He thought he had just closed his eyes,
When, suddenly wide awake,
He saw light stream from star-filled skies.
Did someone give his arm a shake?

He trampled limbs along the way,
But reached the window in the wall.
And through it saw as clear as day,
Sheep and shepherds, a growing sprawl.

The shepherds told how they had heard
The angel choirs, bright as sun,
Deliver heaven's joyful word
That born was God's Anointed One.

Not since the census was proclaimed
Had such great joy welled in his heart,
Rising up, a flood untamed.
The keeper stretched his arms apart,

Then laughed. As rich as purest gold,
His voice alloyed with angel-song,
To sound and echo a thousand-fold;
"Messiah has come!" rang loud and long.

Read it in the Bible: Luke 2:6-7

So, urging on our puzzled sheep,
We gave no further thought to sleep.

Shepherds

Please come my friend, yes, have a seat,
And hear the tale I have to tell
Of how the One, I came to meet.

It had appeared a common night,
Although there was a certain star
That made the sky seem strangely bright.

A calmness passed among the sheep
While they were settling in small groups
And drifting slowly off to sleep.

We shepherds, too, had settled down
To doze and listen through the night,
As we reclined upon the ground.

Then suddenly there rose a gale
That swept away the commonplace
From every hill and sheltered vale.

In the roaring whirlwind's wake,
Came strains of melody profound—
Such music only angels make.

We trembled at the blinding light
And countless voices in the sky
From singing seraphs shining bright.

One angel, high above the slope,
Announced the long awaited birth
Of our Messiah and our Hope.

It filled our hearts up to the brim
That He had sent for shepherds poor
To be the first to worship Him.

So, urging on our puzzled sheep,
We followed as the angels led
And gave no further thought to sleep.

The angels led to Bethlehem,
Where, back behind the largest inn,
We came upon the three of them:

The man who watched us cautiously,
The woman gazing at her son
As He, awake, lay peacefully.

We had not known what we would see
On going to the Promised One,
But what was this? How could it be

That, in a stable, dark and small
And in a manger heaped with straw
Would lie the Savior of us all?

Yet, this was where the angel led
Who told us of Messiah's birth,
So bowing down before His bed,

We knelt. We were able to arise
With certainty that in the straw,
There lay our King before our eyes.

We knew that He would understand
That we had just one thing to give,
And placed our hearts into His hand.

As, to the hills we made our way,
The Child alone was on our minds;
We spoke of nothing else that day.

We will be shepherds our whole lives,
Yet we are changed, for in our hearts
The glory of that night survives.

Read it in the Bible: Luke 2:8-20

He grew shy as he drew near,
Would a shepherd boy be welcomed here?

The Shepherd Boy

Children to the shepherd went
Excitedly to make their plea,
Would he just one more time consent
To tell them of that wondrous night?
Closing his eyes, the memory
Flowed like this before his sight.

Old Jacob, as a boy, was sent
To shepherd all his father's sheep.
Like other shepherds, with no tent,
He learned that lying on the ground
At the sheepfold gate to sleep,
He would hear if threats came around.

Thus, the night that angels came,
Jacob lay in bright starlight
That flickered in the sky like flame.
He heard the trumpet blasts resound,
Announcing choirs left and right,
While they took stations all around.
The other shepherds, too, awoke
As angelic anthems filled the night.
Then one angel neared and spoke,

"Do not fear, we bring to you
News of joy for Israel
That her wait at last is through.
The Messiah, born this night,
With humanity will dwell,
That it with God may reunite."

Running like it was a race,
In the blink of an angel's eye,
Jacob came upon the place.
The shepherd boy, as he drew near,
Slowed, as he suddenly grew shy,
"What if they do not want me here?"

Then the parents stepped aside
And at the manger made some room,
So he approached, eyes opened wide.
There he saw upon the straw,
Like a light dispelling gloom,
The Child who filled his heart with awe.

When Jacob knelt, the Infant raised
A tiny wrinkled hand.
The shepherd boy looked on, amazed,
Then placed his finger in the palm,
And though he did not understand,
His pounding heart grew quiet, calm.

Babies are blind when born, he knew,
Yet, from the manger, those dark eyes
Caught his own and saw right through.
Minutes like a moment passed
And then he rose with stifled sighs,
Making way for those less fast.

They, within the small cave massing,
Before the rough-hewn manger knelt
As rising sun marked night's swift passing.
Returning to flocks up on the hill,
The shepherd boy within him felt
The Newborn's touch and presence still.

Jacob was more than satisfied,
While time slipped by from year to year,
To watch the sheep on this hill side.
Then heaven on the shepherd smiled:
He saw The Teacher drawing near,
And recognized in Him, the Child.

He had to follow, could not stay,
But, that will have to be, I fear,
A tale to tell another day.

Read it in the Bible: Luke 2:8–20

The Magi (Told by Balthazar)

Though some have called us sages,
We merely read the skies
That mutely gaze upon us
With wisdom in their eyes.

Exploring heaven's insight,
We saw the royal star
Proclaim a king of unmatched might
A monarch from afar.

It was a bit confusing;
The message was not clear.
It seemed that He was reigning,
And yet His birth was near.

The star was not to be ignored.
Yes, we stargazers three
Were called to meet this mighty Lord,
And see His majesty.

Aware the journey could be long
And brigands think us prey,
We formed a party fifty strong
And soon got underway.

As dogs, while hunting in a band,
Pursue without a rest,
We, day by day and land by land,
From Persia traveled west.

We tracked the star, a beacon,
Ablaze up in the sky,
But near the River Jordan
It ceased to shine on high.

With Jordan River just behind,
We asked in Jericho,
And they were of a single mind,
"In New Shalom, they'll know."

Our guide no longer lit the skies,
So we proceeded there,
And found a city of good size
With bustle everywhere.

We went before the one who reigned,
King Herod was his name.
He listened, but his face grew pained
On hearing why we came.

The king found in Jerusalem
This answer from the scribes:
"It is the town of Bethlehem
The prophet here describes."

But Herod ordered us to wait,
Then summoned us by night
With urgent questions on the date
The star revealed its light.

If God's Messiah could be found,
The king intended to
Bestow his gift, make trumpets sound
With welcome from each Jew.

"So, when you find God's Holy One,"
Come back and please tell me,"
His voice was warm as morning sun
Which led us to agree.

When Herod said that we could go,
We did not wait for day,
But hurried as the welcome glow
Of starlight showed the way.

It showered light upon the place,
A watch-fire for our sake.
Our party labored at the pace
And fell back in our wake.

We brought our gifts before His throne
And felt a peace before unknown.

A strangely busy town, we found,
And filled with sheep, a horde,
Through which in haste we quickly wound,
By shepherds quite ignored.

We neared a cave carved in a hill;
Had heaven missed its aim?
Or was it true and did it still
His royal birth proclaim?

Remaining distant, yet we saw
The Babe for whom we came,
Within a trough with little straw
To cushion His small frame.

Recalling who the Infant was,
We bowed down very low.
His mother beckoned us because
We hardly dared to go.

At last approaching where He lay,
Wrapped up against the chill,
The question would not go away,
Would He the stars fulfill?

A mighty lord; this humble place;
They seemed to disagree,
But when I saw and touched His face,
I knew the King was He.

We heard our group approaching
And signed for them to stay.
Servants dug out without coaching
The bag brought for this day.

First, Melchior pulled from the pack
His wealth in polished gold.
He did not fear that he might lack
For he was very old.

Young Casper from the bundle took
A crimson leather purse
Of blended incense which he shook
To watch the dust disperse.

And I who write this, Balthazar,
Had felt compelled to bring
A jar of precious myrrh this far,
An odd gift for a king.

But, having firmly grasped the urn,
I signaled to both men
That with our gifts we should return
To honor Him again.

Before the Great King's simple throne,
We knelt and we bestowed.
Our gifts on Him, as peace unknown
Like living waters flowed.

His gentle parents were most kind
And asked if we would stay,
To rest a bit from leagues behind,
Until another day.

That night brought us a troubling dream,
Its message dark and grim
Regarding Herod's bloody scheme;
We could not go to him.

Instead, we chose another way
And hurried from that land,
Discussing all we saw that day
That we might understand.

Read it in the Bible: Matthew 2:1-12

New Testament:

Model of a Disciple's Journey

**Journey to the Font of Mercy
(The Woman Caught in Adultery)**

The temple priests all envied Him,
This man who made the temple home,
Who caused their lights, once bright, to dim,
This man, the talk of New Shalom.
For Jesus taught as none before,
And promised there was something more.

Come morning, Jesus often went
Up to the temple where He taught,
And there a trap for Him was sent
By foes who hoped He would be caught.

While He, the Father's mercy taught,
Some elders dragged a woman, bound,
And Jesus' judgment they besought,
"Behold, this woman we have found

"No one condemns you?" He asked her.
She whispered back, "no, no one sir."

While she was in grave sin's embrace.
By Moses' Law, she should be stoned,
But, Rabbi, will you judge this case?
By mercy is her sin condoned?"

Instead He squatted down to write
A psalm to mercy on the ground.
Again they asked, now less polite,
But still He wrote and made no sound.

The restless crowd around them stood.
At last, He spoke with upraised eyes,
"Let him among you who is good,
Whose heart has felt no evil rise,

The one among you with no sin,
Be first to lift a stone to throw."
The crowd began to look within
And saw what none but God would know.

When Jesus paused to look her way,
He saw her standing there alone.
"Has none condemned you here today?
Has no one thrown at you a stone?"

She answered Him with lowered head
And whispered voice, "no, no one sir."
"Let mercy then from God," He said,
"Flow in where spite and fear once were.

Now, woman, go and sin no more."
She left Him, changed, not as before.

Read it in the Bible: John 8:1–11

Journey to Conversion (Saul)

Saul was a student of the law,
With deep-set eyes ablaze with zeal,
Who bowed before his God with awe,
But with others was less genteel.

Opposing the activity
Of those who followed The Way,
Saul raised his voice most fervently
To preserve God's honor, day by day.

Saul supported Stephen's stoning
That left his body lifeless clay,
For Stephen, by signs and preaching,
Had drawn many to The Way.

With his zeal and fiery passion,
Saul battered down doors to find them.
Some he had held in prison,
As others fled Jerusalcm.

To Damascus Saul was sent
Arresting any he could find
Who to this Christ gave their assent
And faith in One God undermined.

His party traveled through the heat,
Moving northward, day by day.
The trek, at last, was near complete,
Damascus only hours away,

When, startled by a blinding light,
Saul tumbled to the ground.
There, a voice broke through his fright
With a thunderous sound,

"You persecute me, Saul, but why?"
Answered Saul, "Lord, who are you?"
"I am the Jesus you decry.
Go! A messenger will come to you."

With opened eyes, Saul could not see
And had to be led by the hand.
He proceeded uneasily
To Damascus at Jesus' command.

At the home where he was staying,
He found a corner, quiet and still,
Where he sat fasting and praying
That God would soon disclose His will.

In Damascus, members of the sect,
Now calling themselves Christian,
Knew they could, with Saul, expect
Imprisonment or flight again.

To a certain Christian, Ananias,
Three days later came a vision:
To the house of a man named Judas
He was sent with a commission.

He would meet the Christian hater,
Who knelt in prayer both day and night,
Then assure him God is greater
Than a simple lack of sight.

Laying hands upon the man,
He would see Saul's sight restored.
"But, this man," Ananias began.
"He stands against you, Lord.

"It is your church He would destroy,
And even now, so I am told,
He has letters to employ,
That any Christian he may hold."

"Go!" the Lord said in the vision,
"He is to be my instrument,
Enduring anguish and derision,
To take my Word where he is sent."

Scales loosened from his eyes and fell.
"Let me be baptized, as well,"

Ananias, no longer afraid,
To the street named Straight then went
And asked, "Is this where Saul has stayed?
By the Lord I have been sent."

He laid his hands upon Saul's head,
"The Lord has struck you in this way
That all your blindness might be shed
And, in His name, for sight I pray."

Scales loosened from Saul's eyes and fell;
His vision was fully restored.
"Let me be baptized now, as well,
In Barada River," he implored.

Baptized, then to the synagogue;
Within him, the Spirit's fire burned
And, when Saul rose with a monologue,
The focus of his zeal had turned.

He spoke of One who died and rose;
Those who listened were amazed,
"Did he not come arresting those
Who thus believe in Jesus, raised?"

Saul remained for several days
In the city where all could see,
And he clearly argued in many ways
Why God's Christ must Jesus be.

Those who called Saul to the city
Were displeased with what they heard.
They planned his death and made him flee,
But Saul's resolve was undeterred.

As he preached about his Master,
He bore the flag of Christ unfurled,
Facing foe and natural disaster
To bring His message to the world.

Read it in the Bible: Acts of the Apostles 7:54—8:3; 9:1-25

Journey to Integrity (Zacchaeus)

He nearly had not gone to see—
There would be a teeming crowd,
Most of which would like to see
Him wrapped in a burial shroud.

As senior tax collector
For the emperor in Rome,
He was seen as thief, as robber
Of his people and his home.

Zacchaeus, since he was quite small,
Expected elbows in his face,
But he could not resist the call
That drew him to this place.

The Prophet, yes, The Nazarene,
On his way to Jericho—
Amidst the horde he had foreseen,
Massed, hoping for a healing show.

Then, just outside the city,
To a beggar blind from birth,
The Prophet showed respect and pity,
As to a man of worth.

Over the crowd the story flew.
Said Jesus, "Bid him come to me."
Then, "What would you have me do?"
"Please, Lord," he answered, "let me see."

Jesus replied, "Receive your sight.
By your faith you have been saved."
The beggar danced with all his might,
"Praised be God! I see!" he raved.

The Prophet entered Jericho
On the downside of the day,
Curious crowds continued to grow,
Pushing Zacchaeus farther away.

His struggles left him crimson-faced,
With Jesus in the mob somewhere.
The tax man in his mouth could taste
A bitterness born of despair.

Then, he saw a sycamore tree
With arms outstretched for him,
Zacchaeus thought, perhaps, that he
Might see Jesus from a limb.

But, was there any better way?
What about his dignity?
And things those looking on would say
In ungentle mockery?

No other option could he see.
Let the rabble watch and jeer,
He must go and climb that tree,
For Jesus, on the road, drew near.

As, in a cloth, one strand might pass,
With dips and ducks to the other side,
He threaded through the milling mass,
Toward the tree, his goal and guide.

Then, having reached the tree he sought,
He eyed its first limb warily,
For it was higher than he thought;
He scrabbled up, though clumsily.

The crowd seemed as an endless sea,
Spread before the tax man's sight;
Jesus waded through as easily,
As a torch through dark of night.

The small man's heartbeat felt like thunder,
When Jesus walked beneath his limb.
Zacchaeus, then, was struck with wonder;
The Prophet stopped and turned to him.

He hoped that if he climbed that tree,
He might get high enough to see.

He looked the taxman in the eye
And said, "Zacchaeus, come down."
He squeaked out, "Rabbi," in reply,
The height, though, made him frown.

The small man hoped that he could slide
From the tree with dignity,
But his tunic caught, as did his pride.
Down he sprawled, for all to see.

Loud laughter swept across the crowd,
Waves upon this human sea,
Spreading word of the taxman proud,
Tumbling from a sycamore tree.

Zacchaeus, though, remained unbowed.
He caught his breath and stood upright.
Jesus gestured and said aloud,
"I will stay with you tonight."

The waters of the sea transformed:
As Jesus' words passed mouth to ear.
With rising anger, people stormed,
And, in their anger, did not hear

Or see Zacchaeus to Jesus turn,
"With the poor, I split my wealth;
Fourfold, too, will I return
All I have gained by theft or stealth."

Despite the people's castigation,
Jesus raised His voice to say,
"To this man has come salvation,
And likewise to his house this day.

"He once was numbered with the lost,
But he, too, is Abraham's son."
Like white caps that the winds have tossed,
The crowd sprayed angry words as one.

But the tax man walked with Jesus,
Intent on Jesus' every word.
The vile names spewed at Zacchaeus,
All drifted by him, never heard.

The mob walked to the tax man's gate,
But the two showed no reaction.
The crowd began to dissipate,
Which left the pair without distraction.

The morning brought a new life view,
With The Prophet, he would go;
But Jesus said, "I have for you
Work to do in Jericho."

Changed because he heeded the call:
Though bodily still stout and short,
Compassion made him seem more tall—
A big man of another sort.

For many years, all those in need
Of comfort and aid could go
To the taxman once un-treed,
When Jesus came to Jericho.

Read it in the Bible: Luke 18:35 — 19:10

With the Spirit flowing from the skies,
God's hand will save the one who cries
Upon the Lord with lifted eyes.

Journey to Church
(The Elamite Tells his Story)

From Susa, many leagues I came,
Because I sought the Living God,
Whose voice had called the Jews by name.
A quest like mine should not seem odd,
"The Living God is not the same
As gods the other nations claim."

That morning, I, an Elamite,
Was in the temple when, nearby,
I saw a startling flash of light,
When flame flowed from a fractured sky,
And through the city roared with might.
Then, at a house, it slowed its flight,

And glowed as if to beckon me.
What God had done so long before
For Moses with the burning tree,
He did with sacred fire once more,
That filled the house entirely,
Consuming nothing we could see.

We wondered what this sign could be,
But there was more, for we could hear,
With accents born in Galilee,
Men's voices raised as one, so clear,
And in such languages that we
All understood them easily.

Out on the lower roof, a man,
With tongues of flame upon his head,
Called out, "The prophet showed God's plan,
'God sends His Spirit.' Joel said."
And so The Fisherman began,
With words from God, not those of man.

I watched the crowd increase in size,
While Peter spoke of final days:
The Spirit flowing from the skies;
The heavens with dread signs ablaze;
And God's hand saving him who cries
Upon the Lord with upraised eyes.

Like one with secrets to confide,
His softened voice drew us ahead,
"The man called Jesus traveled wide,
His wondrous works and words," he said.
"The Father's love exemplified,
For He and God as one abide.

"But Jesus you then crucified,
As was permitted by God's plan.
The grave held grimly Him Who died,
Yet only for a two-day span.
The sealing stone was rolled aside,
But Jesus, raised, was not inside.

"This Jesus Whom you crucified,
Has God made now both Christ and Lord,
As David's Psalms had testified."
Our hearts were cut as by a sword.
"What must we do?" some of us cried,
To which The Fisherman replied,

"Repent of all your sins today
And in the waters, be baptized."
These things I did without delay.
My journey's goal was realized,
And I remain until this day
A true disciple of the Way.

Read it in the Bible: Acts of the Apostles 2

Andrew found a lad who said
That he would share five loaves of bread.

Journey to the Lord's Table
(Told by John the Apostle)

"Dear children, does it really seem
There is no work for me to do?"
Said John with voice and visage stern.
The old man's eyes, though, held their gleam.
"Alright, a short one, known to you,
That still has truths for us to learn."

Close by the Sea of Galilee,
We walked and listened carefully,
Afraid to miss a single word
Because we savored all we heard.

Upon us came a clamoring crowd
Who wondered at His works aloud
And thought, in Jesus, they might see
The One ordained to set them free.

While Jesus sat and taught all day,
More people came, none slipped away.
On Philip's face, He saw dismay
That we lacked means with which to pay

For food enough to feed them all,
The sun's decline he could not stall.
But Jesus did not hesitate
And, even though it had grown late,

He said to feed those gathered there
Who had no food they could prepare.
Then, Andrew found a lad who said
That he would share five loaves of bread.

They were quite small, as were two fish,
"Please take and share these if you wish."
The young man offered without guile.
His grin replied to Jesus' smile.

Then, Jesus blessed the fish and bread,
And added, "See that all are fed."
When their dining was complete,
We gathered all they did not eat,

We ended with twelve baskets filled.
The crowd, now having this need stilled,
Had little doubt what they should do,
"Proclaim Him king," the voices grew.

To their desires, He could not yield;
It was not time to be revealed.
He, knowing this, sent us away,
And up the mountain went to pray.

The night brought us one more surprise,
When Jesus walked before our eyes,
Right on the surface of the sea.
We could not tell that it was He.

We thought, instead, we saw a ghost
And we were still far from the coast.
He saw our anguish and moved near,
"It is I, children. Do not fear."

"If it is You, Lord," Peter cried,
"Beckon me out to your side."
"Come" said Jesus. Peter leapt,
And on the water safely stepped.

The wind was making waves as high
As you are tall, my young Eli.
Well, Peter feared and turned his eye
From Jesus to the waves and sky.

Waves grabbed his legs; he gave a shout
To Jesus who, then, reaching out,
Plucked Peter from the now calm sea.
His disappointment we could see,

"So little faith. Why did you doubt?"
Words, too, for us who did not get out.
Yet, we expressed our faith as one,
And cried, "You truly are God's Son!"

In the boat I was not alone,
But our faith since then has grown
In Peter's place, what would you do?
And, also, let me ask of you,

Was it by chance, do you think,
The choice to act in faith or sink
Came after Jesus blessed the bread
And by it we had all been fed?

Read it in the Bible: John 6:1-15;
Matthew 14:22-33

**Journey through Death to New Life
(Lazarus, Told by Martha and Mary)**

We welcome you, Mary and I,
As does our brother, Lazarus,
Whose story Pharisees deny
And over which the priests all fuss.

It happened just three months ago.
Our brother had a dizzy spell,
Infirmity then knocked him low.
When he failed to soon get well,

Twenty messengers we sent
To every desert, valley, hill,
Finding Jesus our intent,
With word, "The one you love is ill."

(Her sister, Mary, spoke from there).
Found at last alone in prayer,
He listened to the herald's word;
From Jesus, His disciples heard.

"Our friend, Lazarus is ill,"
Said Jesus coming down the hill.,
"But with death it will not end.
Instead God's glory will ascend."

Two days more, He chose to take,
Then said to them, "I must awake
Lazarus who is asleep."
They looked at Him blank-eyed like sheep.

"Will he not wake up on his own?"
Asked one desiring to postpone
A trip to where the Pharisees
Would, if they could, their Master seize.

So Jesus turned and plainly said,
"Our dear friend Lazarus is dead,
But God's glory will be manifest."
He turned again and westward pressed.

When news arrived of Jesus, near,
We had to greet Him, that was clear.
But with the mourners, one must stay,
So I sent Martha on her way.

(Martha took that as her cue),
"Jesus, you have come to us!"
I called when He came into view.
"But my brother, Lazarus,

"With you here, would not have died.
Still, now, if You pray, God will hear."
"But, he will rise," the Lord replied.
"Do not surrender to that fear."

"Yes, on the final day he will,"
I answered, but He turned to me,
And when He spoke, I felt a chill,
"All those with open eyes shall see

"And know: I am The Resurrection."
As we conversed, we walked the road
In Bethany's direction.
We reached the outskirts; Jesus slowed.

(She to Mary then gave way).
I hoped that I could slip away
When Martha came and said that He
Wished to wait and speak to me.

Some friends and mourners saw me leave
And thought I left the house to grieve.
They planned to follow to the grave,
But saw I went not to that cave.

To the Jericho Road I went.
And brought to Jesus my lament
That Lazarus need not have died,
But words escaped me and I cried.

With a voice that rang about,
He commanded, "Lazarus, come out."

The Lord's eyes, too, filled up with tears,
As troubled questions reached our ears,
"The blind man's sight, He could renew,
Why could He not heal this man, too?"

Some moments later, lifting His head,
"Where have you laid him?" He softly said.
I took His hand, saying, "Come and see."
We went on into Bethany.

(Martha then took up the story).
I heard voices drawing near
And watched the path into the quarry,
Knowing soon they would appear.

We stood as one before the grave;
I saw wet trails run down His face.
Jesus gestured with a wave,
"Move the stone back from its place."

For Lazarus, in his thick rock womb,
Lay sealed by a massive stone.
I said, "Four days within the tomb,"
"Surely now a stench has grown."

"Did I not say that you would see
And know the glory of your God?"
He gently said, reminding me.
Men moved the stone upon my nod.

Then Jesus lifted up His eyes,
"You, Father, always hear My plea.
I speak that these may realize
And come to trust that You sent Me."

He looked out at the open tomb,
And with a voice that rang about
Like echoes in an empty room,
Commanded, "Lazarus, come out."

We felt the whole world catch its breath,
All held as by an iron band,
Until, loosed from the grip of death,
My brother answered this command.

(Mary touched her brother lightly),
Leg and body cloths wrapped tightly
Made Lazarus fall to the ground.
Jesus called, "Let him be unbound."

All present there were filled with awe,
But quickly some took what they saw
Back to the priests and Pharisees
Who wallow in their jealousies.

Thus they made things quite hard for us,
With lies concerning Lazarus.
They planned the death of Jesus, too,
Who did as He had come to do.

The priestly envy satisfied
When they saw Jesus crucified,
Became astounded disbelief,
As Jesus, raised, relieved our grief.

Seen by many through forty days,
He rose heavenward before our gaze
And now He sits at God's right side;
His Spirit still will be our guide.

Read it in the Bible: John 11:1-54

Your Journey

In his second letter to Timothy, Paul writes, "All scripture is inspired by God and is of value for teaching, for criticizing and correcting errors, and for guiding us in the way we ought to live." (2 Timothy 3:16, paraphrased). *Journeys* is a collection of stories, but the stories are rooted in scripture. They are like the moon; while it is not the source of light, but only its reflector, it is still able to guide us through the dark night.

Believers in Jesus as the Anointed One of God might want to use these stories to shed light on their life journey. If this applies to you, I would consider it a privilege and an honor if you would permit me to provide some small measure of assistance.

I am preparing a set of exercises based on the stories in *Journeys* (available by January, 2011). The exercises may be used individually or within the context of a family or small church group.

Each of the seventeen exercises has the following structure:
1. Take a few minutes to let go of the concerns of the day and place yourself in the presence of God.
2. Read the specified poem from *Journeys*, preferably aloud since that is when poetry is at its best.
3. Think about and respond to a question related to the poem.
4. Read a specified passage from the Bible, consisting of, or related to one of the stories.
5. Reflect on the passage in the stillness of your heart.
6. Read a few thoughts on one aspect of the passage.
7. Reflect and respond to two questions. This may be done alone, perhaps in a journal to be reread or shared later with a small group or spiritual advisor, or the reflection and responses may be oral, done in the context of a small group.
8. Close with a prayer. I provide one that you may use and make your own.

For a specific example, see the exercise for Noah that follows on page 107.

I do not intend to make money on the meditations. However, my cost to make and mail one copy, in the United States in 2010, is about $3.00. If you would like a copy and are able to do so, I would welcome a donation to cover that expense.

I will honor any request, regardless of whether it includes a donation. Any donations in excess of costs will be donated to serve the Church.

I grant permission to make copies of the exercises as needed with the following qualifications.
- All copies must include the copyright page in its entirety
- If you make changes in the document, excluding typographical and grammatical corrections, please note them on the copyright page (front or back). If changes are extensive, please do me the courtesy of sending me a copy of the revised document.
- If you distribute copies to others, you may charge no more than your actual copying and distribution expenses.

To obtain a copy of exercises for your journey, send your name and mailing address to
    Steve Gannaway
    c/o The Maine Seasons
    12 Lucerne St.
    Springvale, ME   04083
    maine.seasons@hotmail.com

Landmark One: Mount Ararat

1. Take a little time to settle your spirit, calm your mind, relax your body, and rest in the knowledge that the Creator of the Universe has come to spend this time with you.
2. Read "Journey to Mount Ararat (Noah)" in *Journeys*, out loud if possible.
3. The poem does not address the nature of the evil on earth. We may assume, though, that Noah's behavior was in sharp contrast to the behavior of the rest of humankind. Since behavior reveals a person's character, revisit the poem to identify and list the character traits that Noah possessed. Which of these traits do you possess? How do your actions reveal these character traits?
4. Read Genesis 8: 13-22
5. Listen with your heart to the words you just read.
6. Consider this. Our society encourages an "It's all about me" attitude, but this story reminds us that it is not all about us. In the story, it is not about the flood, nor is it about those who died or survived. It certainly is not about rainbows. Rather, "It is all about God." It always has been and always will be. It is about obedience to God's commands, about waiting for God's time, about God's mercy.

7. Reflect and respond to these questions.
    a. Noah incurred the ridicule of people in the region by obeying God and building a huge boat, probably in a forest, far from water. Think of a time that you felt that you should do something, risking the ridicule of others. Perhaps, telling someone that Jesus loves them or that you would pray for them, backing up someone who was unpopular, or standing for a principle. Did you take the risk? Afterward, how did you feel about doing or not doing it?
    b. Noah insisted on thanking God before moving from the ark and returning to the world. Along your journey what are/should you be grateful for? Make a list and keep it in a place where you will be sure to see it every day. Each time you see it, take time to express that gratitude to God. Even a simple, "Thank you, God" is enough.
8. Pray: Father in heaven, thank you for your goodness and generosity toward me. I thank You especially for getting me through the storms I encounter along my journey. It is not that you let me avoid them, but that their winds and waves, as great as they may be, are never more fierce than You have prepared me to meet. Help me to celebrate and express gratitude for each rainbow You send to let me know that You have not forgotten me.

www.ingramcontent.com/pod-product-compliance
Lightning Source LLC
Chambersburg PA
CBHW031404040426
42444CB00005B/414